ECHOES FROM THE DARK

A CATHARTICUM
WHERE STRUGGLE FINDS VOICE
AND SILENCE FINDS RELEASE

BY

Walter R Davidson-West

"It's not what happens to you, but how you react to it that matters,"

EPTICTETEUS

This is my purge, my version of letting that shit go.

"Circumstances don't make the man, they only reveal him to himself".

EPICTETEUS

TABLE OF CONTENTS

INTRODUCTION

This book has two purposes—kind of like a Swiss Army knife for the soul.

First, it's personal. A cathartic act. My way of cracking open the bottle of emotions and thoughts that I usually shove into the back of the mental fridge only to find them years later, stale and leaking. Writing is how I keep myself from exploding. When life gets loud, messy, or straight-up absurd, I run to the pen. It's my weapon of choice—no bullets, just ink. Through it, I've wrestled with my emotions, my logic, my spirit, and the slippery concepts of right, wrong, reality, and whatever society thinks it's serving us this week. What you'll find here is not every thought I've ever had (thank God), but rather glimpses into the darkness and the light that comes from staring into it too long.

Second, it's for you. My hope is that when you put this book down, something shifts—maybe just a fraction, maybe a seismic shake. You don't have to agree with me (half the time I don't even agree with myself). You don't have to "get it." But if my words nudge you toward a new perspective—on yourself, on others, on the social traps we walk into daily—then this book has done its job.

Now, I owe thanks. To the warriors of wisdom who stand guard at the gates, fighting against the negative forces woven deep into our collective being—thank you. Without your light, I'd have been lost in the fog long ago. You know who you are, both here in the flesh and in the spirit realm. And for those curious to dive deeper, I'll leave a breadcrumb trail: a handful of thinkers, teachers, and creators I follow on YouTube, who continue to challenge my mind and expand my soul.

So, with gratitude and a dash of audacity, I hand you this book. May it be both a mirror and a magnifying glass—revealing, distorting, provoking, and, hopefully, transforming.

ACKNOWLEDGEMENT & DISCLAIMER

·———⟨◦⟩———·

*B*efore you dive deeper: a quick but important note. The poems and opinions in this book are my voice — not the voice of anyone I mention below. The authors, historians, and online teachers I list here did not write this book, and these pages should not be read as their official views. This section is my homage — a thank-you to the great minds and creators who sharpened my thinking, challenged my assumptions, and helped me hold my perspective together.

Authors (also searchable on YouTube):
John G Jackson, John Henrick Clark, Dr. Yosef Ben Jochannan, Ivan Van Sertima, Ronoko Rashidi, Amos Wilson, Dr. James Smalls, Dr. Lila Africa, Chancellor Williams, Joseph Murphy, David Hawkins, Maxwell Maltz, Ra Un Nefer Amern, Earnest Holmes, James Allen, Charles Haanel, — and many more whose work has been part of my intellectual and spiritual unfolding.

YouTube personalities I follow:
Kurimeo Ahau, Anoymousparty, Brother Rich from Blackmagik363, ReelNagas, Aseer the Duke of Tiers, Dane Calloway, Kt the Arch Degree, Yahki Awakened, Dr. Umar, Phil Valentine, Don Kilam, Blue Pill, Red Pill — among others who keep the conversation sharp and provocative.

I turn to all of these voices not to copy them, but to keep my perspective whole and avoid becoming fragmented. Their books, lectures, and videos helped me navigate a world that often treats me like an outsider — teaching me to see patterns, question narratives, and locate the invisible structures shaping our lives. If anything in these pages echoes something you've heard from one of them, that's because their teachings helped refine the lens through which I look — not because they endorse or own these exact words.

Finally: call it what you will — a matrix, a racket, a cultural fog — but my reading and listening made one thing painfully clear: distortion, lies, and suppression have been the quiet weapons used to warp our reality. Everyday people of all backgrounds are the hypothetical victims of that unseen assault. This book is one small attempt to identify

the distortions and, maybe, start shedding a little light.

MY FIRST LOVE

I remember – Vaguely

Hazily

Sitting on the floor –at 3 possibly 4

Me -now forty plus seven scores—I remember

Maybe—technically just a baby

On the floor

Playing with toys before she went out the door

My first love- going out the door

A chore easy to ignore

I was none the wiser --she had done it a thousand times before

I'm sure—I remember her

Out to the store for what I can now imagine was regret

Betrayal—Loss

Abandonment—Addiction

Shame and Disrespect

In the form of a cigarette.

But I remember—how could I forget

I was lost—my first love –lost

I remember

At 3 possibly 4, sitting on the floor playing with toys—little brother not far from me

When she left—went out the door

In fact

I'm sure she had done it a thousand times before

But this time she

She couldn't come back.

THE BUG (ARMAGEDDON)

As One day draws to an end

The dawn of another will soon begin

Dead men walk to the earth's end

Puzzled minds and faces

Cry and laugh in the aftermath of what happened

Dead bodies scattered across rocky terrains

Millions walk emotionlessly with no brains

Silence echoes throughout

Billions of towns and streets

No more love, no more victory,

Just defeat

Times passes as 30 seconds feels like 30 days

Many trapped by the devil's eye

And some engorged by his flames

Who's the blame

No one–after the clock strikes 12

Nothing will ever be the same

Puzzled minds and faces cry to the tune of what happened

7

What did happen was

Blood shed

And guns clapped, grounds covered with

Dead republicans and dead democrats

Disaster struck

Man, only given the option of death

So, who gives a fuck about...

What happened to

All the sandy beaches and busy streets

Who cares about waterfalls and fly new sneaks?

Cause they gone

Gone,

Gone with the days of our lives

What happed to the self-proclaimed nation?

Built around killers and common thieves

That never settled for defeat

Weak.

What happened

As shorty gazes at this cesspool, we once called life

Now he can only dream about what could have been

Never to experience a lover

Or a friend

What happened

Was no alarm can stop the impact of an atomic bomb

Hold on, be strong, it won't take long

Listen

I know you hear it, silent whispers, his footsteps

Cold chills, as death enters

The world is finished

All signs of life diminished

What happened was love was completely conquered

By hate

The millennium bug struck

But we were too late.

12/31/99 @11:57PM

BEAUTY'S THOUGHT

I am everything you see and

Everything you cannot

The yin and the yang

The blistering cold and the smoldering hot

I am the wind beneath and behind your wings,

I am the reason the birds hum and sing,

I am the rising sun at dawn

And the setting sun at dusk

I am the ivory in the elephants' tusks.

I am everything you see and

Everything you cannot

The yin and the yang

The blistering cold and the smoldering hot

I am the clouds up above

I am your heart and soul

I am your love

I am the ocean crashing against the sand

I am evolution

I am the mere existence of wo and man

I am the mystery of the ancient world

I am a baby

Whether it be a boy or a girl

I am the love you feel

When you think of each other

The conversations on the phone

I am the burning passion you feel deep within

When you are all alone

I am everything you see and

Everything you cannot

The yin and the yang

The blistering cold and the smoldering hot

I am for no apparent reason

I am the four seasons

I am the night and the day

I am the universe

I am a woman at the moment she gives birth

I am the snow and the rain that

Raps, beats rapidly and covers windowpanes

I am forever

I am the reason you never say never

I am the sizzling scene in which kids play

I am the roses that bloom

On a breezy spring afternoon

I am the reason wolves howl at the moon

I am pure

But am I white?

Yes

Am I wrong or am I right?

I am everything you see and

Everything you cannot

The yin and the yang

The blistering cold and the smoldering hot

I am the death of a loved one

I am history

I am fun

I am that sparkle in her eyes

Which twinkle like diamonds and pearls

I am the illuminations of the sun and stars that shine bright

I am the feeling of victory after a long hard fight

I am, by definition, quality pleasing to the eye

Am I or aren't I

To be or not to be

I am black

I am beauty

BURDENED WITH HOPE

I want to see your mind

Completely naked

Stripped down to its barest essence

As we engage in verbal intercourse

At the mercy of this cosmic force—that

Pushes down

Fully submerging our extremities and consciousness

Into a lingual discourse

Until we can't

Until we pant

As we rant—vigorously

Before erupting in silence—

That mesmerizes us with its deafening loudness

And time becomes timeless—

Lost in each other's irises...

Euphoric hormones secrete

As level rises

The intensity of touching without

Actually

Keeps my heart pumping rapidly,

So naturally

You've captured me

Like an insect—with your web of wet intellect

I could never lose interest in

In your subtext

The panoramic pictures you've constructed and painted

Forces me to take everything into perspective and context,

Firing up the engines of my Imagination-

That pleasantly restructure my mental configuration and

Released my desire

Displacing old woes

and

Filled my inner self with a blazing fire –

I am branded

Hanging on your every word

I have landed

On cloud 9 to the 3rd

Your seeds have already rooted and have taken hold

Of what's left of my soul

I must confess ---Yes ---you are --the absolute best

So,

Let's get old

Better yet

We should elope

See

From the moment you spoke

You burdened me with

Hope

LIVE

Life is beautiful

From insects to hair follicles

From parasites to cuticles

From cool and calm summer nights to the hot intensity of work
cubicles

The world is painted with divine images

Sharing the same air and molecules

A myriad of colors and personalities

That gives life character—and depth—and deep breaths,

Spliffs, whips, hot chicks, played over a wicked guitar riff—and

Still, we don't stop to take a whiff,

Admire or appreciate the gifts

We'd rather

Rape, maim, and kill

Rather than heal, inspire, and uplift

Instead of cultivating the openness of one consciousness spread
out across individuals—We,

Approach everything with 2 clinched fists

We resist

The beauty that life has to offer—either

Because moms was a crack head and or pops wasn't around—he chose not to be bothered,

And still flowers bloom—in concrete gardens

While grass grows on top of coffins

Even when you believe you starving

Heavy rains fall—

Seeds are sown and bear fruit

You don't have to listen

To witness truth,

The sun sets and rises

Whether or not you realize it's

Majesty

Before, during, and after tragedy

-which when taken in perspective is only a formality—or

A result there of

Or failure to accept—this present

So, it casually eats deep into your hard shell like a cavity

YOUR THOUGHTS—YOUR VISION—WHEN OVERTAKEN

By dark clouds and fog—are the only true casualties

You see

light bends reflecting through and stains your optical lens with
images—and

Whatever it is you think you see

The mind finishes

From rainbows to blemishes

From frolicking fields to maximum STATE penitentiaries

To being rich

To being poor

From cardboard boxes to mansions

From major cities to dirt roads, and back woods

From streams to oceans

Life's beauty never diminishes

Life is beauty and beauty is life—

SO LIVE IT

THE REAL

Endless nights lead to endless days

Foolish thoughts lead to foolish ways

Uncertainty is the plague of all plagues

As sunny days fade into rainy days

Heat swelters the surface of my skin

Bubbling like hot lava

The contents deep within

Then—stop

Then start

As my heart skips 7 thousand beats—after beat, after beat

Am I weak?

Or am I deceased?

As my eyes focus on the sunset

From the edge of the beach across the sea

Somewhere around the horizon

Where the sun used to be

Beautiful dawn or maybe its dusk

My eyes should have long since fell out

From the burning lust

Stop—stop

But time never does, it never will

Stop—

Then I ask

When did it begin or when shall I start, when did I start?

Better yet how does it end, when will I end, how will I end

Or did I, or do I, or am I

Real.

LABELS

When did labels become staples?

For defining oneself, myself, yourself, ourselves---

Us—its

Not how the creator designed us

We

Should not allow labels to define

Who we are, who we were, or who we shall become,

-like

Poor, rich, ugly, beautiful, black, white, African, Asian, good and bad

Are just words

—like

Adjectives, slapped on the outside of,

To describe an idea

To – illicit a response of

Joy, desire, disgust, patriotism, or

Illicit fear,

We're

–trapped in a vortex of mispronounced syllables

Which produce unbalanced verbs, and disconnected colloquial

And the proverbial, and the metaphorical, and the allegorical---
are taken literal

---and it's criminal, and political,

In your face and subliminal,

Messages

Producing genetically modified, toxic growth—on this global
word farm

Keeping the constituency dumb, deaf, blind and confused

Abused—and engaged

By this intricate conundrum of misleading sentences and phrases

Like foreplay-

That keeps us turned up and turned on in an orgy of word porn,

That seems to culminate as a state of pseudo-euphoric mental
ecstasy,

That only serves to stifle minds intellectually

With the deepest complexity

disrespectfully

So, we can't think

--- Straight, or in circles

So, we the rabbit hole plunge deeper

Collectively

Conjoined like name brand twins

To the invisible clouds and wireless underground cables

Until we

Become the embodiment of the stereotypes

Spawned by these

superimposed

Labels....

INSTANT GRATIFICATION

Instant gratification

Leads to instant elation or

Inflammation or a brand-new creation

Of life, romance, or demonization

Creating either bliss or destruction of a once copasetic human relation

Born before, during and after

A few minutes of tissue expansion, copulation and dilation///-- From

Instant gratification

Can spawn bodily relaxation, deep mental contemplation, or

Destroy worlds like revelations,

Jealousy and false implications, baffling minds

Causing misinterpreted information

Where the truth ends up only being a deviation, reproducing itself in subtle variations

Instant gratification

Can lead to happy homes, broken homes, healthy living

Or shattered bones

Moments that are breath taking or mind breaking or induce a

Physical or metaphorical, incarceration

Because we want to be instantly gratified—There is no short supply of

Love, war, togetherness, divorce,

Comfort, and remorse,

Marriage, children, alimony, and child support,

Life, death, lows, highs, and poverty,

Fruitfulness, prosperity, disparity, cloudiness, and clarity—

Disease, weed, liquor, smoking, heaven, and hell,

Degradation, aggravation, constipation,

Soul disintegration, and heart palpitations—

Can all be created from one moment of

Instant gratification.

THE ROAD

To me the phrase, 'Look how far we've come or came"
Is nothing but a fucking slap in the face/See
We used to be or presumed to be/

So called slaves now we neck deep in this rat race,
Still running in place

And

giving constant chase to the shiny Shit ... They dangle in front of
our face,

Like just because we had a black president and
You've replaced master and slave with
Employer and job
everything supposed to be just great...

Like our low median incomes,

Disproportionately poor communities, hunger, fleeting health,

and the not so random acts of violence are just fake....

I mean

It's all in our heads and
We safe....
Yet and still...we
Free falling
Going downhill ...trying to the pump breaks ...to

Stop the bleeding
Before it's too late,

and the book is thrown, as we CATCH another case....

Or another son is murdered—or

Another daughter is raped,

We—used to be great now we MARCH with hopes of saving face...

And this shit is on repeat

At a steady pace

To be honest

Like it's been going on for more than a hundred years

And that's being modest

Every decade, of every year, every month, every second of every day, of every week

Sometimes

At night I lay awake

Going back and forth over the debate –

I ask myself does the term progress really deserve a place

Or is someone just good with paint,

Making everyone believe this shit is something that it ain't

See

I'll never claim that our culture is full of saints

But what I will say is

The sanctity and godliness of society, as a whole, is pretty fucking faint,

I'm not being sarcastic

Just giving it to you straight

see

The fact that inflation is sky high, people are still homeless and starving

And education is 3rd rate

While there are people still out here propagating the gospel of hate

If this is the same type of bulshit that was going on when this country was framed

Its real damn shame

That after all these years.... This is how far we have came.

GOD SLIME

I am

Poetically and genetically

Modified and designed

To give birth to the Neos

Lost in this

Neo medieval, cyberpunk-ish

Transhuman

Pseudo reality matrix like paradigm

To

Reshape the clay, the puddy

The cosmic goo, that is us—is you

To

Reconfigure the

Actions and perspectives

During these so called abysmal biblical times

To

Recalibrate the minds

Deceived by the sound waves of deceptive cons,

Weaving a sophisticated web that keeps you occupied and blind

Until I—we

Reinsert the galactic cube of energon

And your hibernating soul light

That activates your

Universal program

Restarts and comes back online

Then

The truth flashes before your optics

Like a jumbo Megatron

Auto---magically transforming us

So, our intrinsic

Internal cosmic systems operate optimally

Prime

Uncrossing the wires of communication

Between us and the sublime

Unencumbering the microbes of information

That travels through the crown

Connecting us to the source

Funnels down below

And slithers back up your spine

To reveal that

We are sub atomically divine.

I mean

We are in context

Unrefined refined **god slime**

Synthesized into little light bodies

Chromosomes n molecules meshed

Then manifested as flesh

(oh yes)

We are psychosomatic -in kind

We are

All at once the god mind,

In a

Symbiotic relationship

Resonating-in harmony-like numbers

And musical notes like sounds

Fluid matter and time (and)

Once realized

You can shatter those glass ceilings

And erase all lines

Disintegrating those socially constructed earth binds

See

The truth for most of you

In what I'm saying is--- hard to find

You can't imagine life without those chaotic emotions that come with

Myopic views and pseudo dystopic bell chimes

Serving to reinforce your bonds

In fact

The beauty of chaos is

It gives you a background and subtext on which to disappear or to shine

Even when life seems like it's on the decline

And you feel like you want to resign

Remember that when

Darkness falls on one side of the earth

The sun in all its glory

Still manages to shine

And that light

Those rays of delicate information

Are a sign

For the dreamer, the sleeper to awaken

Fellow reflections

It's been time

And in time

As the dormant power bestowed

Emerges from the deep and grows

Into wisdom washing over your soul

Furthering your insight and

That dim kaleidoscope of vibrant colors that is you

Will crystallize and be more defined

Then in time

You can turn your own waters into wine

Stop, pause, and rewind

I said in time

You can turn your own waters into wine

Let that sink in

And absorb it in your core like enzymes

And let nothing distract you

Politics, carnal desires, nor crime

Understand

Nothing you see is really there

And what is

Isn't yours or mine

Force your perception inside

So, all of who you are can finally combine

You won't have to believe

You will know that

The kingdom of heaven is in you

Just pluck the fruit from its vine....

ONCE UPON A TIME

Once upon a time

I was told I was an African

Because of my kinky hair, full lips,

And black skin

I was told, I was dragged kicking and screaming from one land

And brought to another

In shackles-under duress

At the bottom of huge no-named ships

While

Covered in shit (human defecation) and piss

Called a negro and a slave

Then forced to work

Under the threats of death

In large fields being patrolled by

Pale faced men with guns and whips

Until

Something changed

And I was set free only to remain

Taking my so-called master's name

Then

Harassed, ostracized, terrorized, vilified, and hanged

By

Uniformed shields, and white hooded gangs

Evers, King, X, and more slain

Now

All we could pass down was

This embedded idea of generational suffering and victimization

Anger and pain

So

Emotionally fed up and drained we

Got together and formed gangs

For protection and other things

But it was infiltrated

I meant backfired

Led astray by those who never knew freedom

Only the concept of obey

Having the Gaul to betray

Misdirecting with misdirection

so

The reemergence of greatness gradually fell into decay

We became addicted to the fast lane

Which birthed a self-inflicted insurrection

In the form of greed and death

Placing more value on material things and social positions

Instead of family and self,

But

There has to be a connection

Using misinformation and education

I meant indoctrination

As a weapon

Which

Forced me into a state of meditative introspection

That sent me

Back in time

Traveling through the centuries of history with

Analytical dissection

And it was scary

I wasn't prepared for what I found

My-us, our history

Literally buried under mounds

Of menticide, and mounds of physical & paper genocide

And I cried—like a newborn leaving the safety of the womb

I cried

Because I realized

I am not nor have I ever been an African

I have never been that misnomer of a crayon color

Black

In fact

More like a copper-color (Indian) being

Forced to abdicate their lands

Through trickery and infiltration

By Europeans that probably looked just like me

Forced to flea

Looking for freedom from their own persecution

Under some misguided delusion

That eventually became a part of this ruse like illusion

And while wading through the confusion

I realized

It was them not me that sailed on boats like dories

From the beyond the sea

And they were hungry

So, we fed them

Taught them how to survive and accepted them as bredren

Merging our families with them

So, my name has always been

My name

Then came the debauchery

So, we fought

Ultimately

We were culturally assimilated

But we fought

Becoming subjugated and from ancestral lands

Excommunicated

As time lapsed memories faded

We went from autochthon

To Indians

To natives

To negro,

To mulattos, mustees, and mestizos

To black

Shipped all over the map

Forced into ghettos

And strung out on crime and crack

They—we

Turned our sacred chants and dances

To booty shaking and rap

With lost history

Misidentified pride

We are our ancestor's misery

Feuding amongst each other in futility

With no plan

To reclaim what was taken

Understand if you can

I, we, most of us are

Original autochthon born Americans

Now

I know for some of you

This is a hard pill to swallow

Crossing some mental and emotional lines

But think about it

And what it really implies

Because in reality

The truth is

Once upon a time...

They lied.

TERMINOLOGY

Mythological – mythology

Slowly injected into the bloodstream

Like 80's street phlebotomy

Distorting logic –illogically

Surgically

Interwoven into the fabric

The visual optics

The very thoughts of modern-day society,

Diabolically

Hidden between the lines

With the usage of forgotten linguistic etymology

And camouflaged with plain sight symbology

Formally integrated into

Frequency emitting technology

Convoluting

One's ability to recognize the dichotomy,

And

Suppressing the growth of our physical and metaphysical biology

Poisoned food, air, tv, and music

Poisoned everything—its

Pharmacology to

Reconfigure the innate functions of our so-called human DNA

Anatomy and physiology

To disrupt and disconnect

The universal outer god feed

From the base god flow

Coursing inside of yee

So, we

Never identify our identities cosmically

Now

How do we

Break free

From the invisible chains wrap-locked around our brains

In this 1984 futuristic-ish

Zombie like transcontinental global colony

That's

Slowly but surely diminishing life's quality

How do we

Reverse the adverse reverse psychology

Brutally spoon fed to us since birth

Without Vaseline or an apology

Got us basically

Basing reality on make believe

Making us believe

True power exists in a vacuum

In everything outside of we

Or that

Jesus Christ was just a glitch in the matrix

Like some anomaly

Somebody's

Doing everything, they can to

Suppress us all subconsciously

Honestly

Common sense isn't common or

Maybe it just has to be used more commonly

In order to bypass the program

That

Overrides any ideas we have of self-reliance and autonomy

See

I used to think history was the answer

But they intentionally fucked up the chronology

From slave ship narratives

Way back to Europe Greeks, romans, Ethiopia, and the Ptolemies

Distorting facts with half truths

From genesis

Acts, and Deuteronomy

Distracting the masses

With fear, sports, democracy

Demonology and pneumatology

Compounded with legalese

So,

The only way to pull back the veil, on a massive scale

Is to be versed in bull shitology

They

Redefining evolution and ecology

Made us the #1 product

In the economy

The internet is the new tower of babel

It's sociology

Compartmentalizing

The science of self and wisdom

Into confusing titles like

Religion, new age, astrology, and numerology

And it bust down even more

Into different layers of ethics and philosophy

Spread across different arcane doctrines and modalities

Showing divide and conquer

Works as the fundamental base

For all their stratology

Either way

We must

Become acquainted with epistemology

Because all will be revealed when we understand the

Meaning and usage of

Terminology....

TRANSFORMAT---ION

My stagnation is caused by

A deprivation

A hungerless starvation

That's been

Restricting my growth and maturation

While stifling my concentration

And simultaneously killing my motivation

To excel

I've fell and failed

Mainly because

I've retained years of the wrong information

Intravenously given

In a myriad of combinations

Until I caught

The cyclical redundant, bigoted, and greedy nature of the
machine in mid rotation,

So, I began to search

For a sense of understanding and mental emancipation

Somehow surviving

An onslaught of physical assaults and psychological
manipulation

Resulting in sensory and psychosomatic devastation

That has proliferated

Generation after insignificant generation

A sort of covert/overt operation

Directly and indirectly aimed

At all sections of the population

Through social and economic castration and strangulation

While we are distracted by

Who's winning, pandemics,

And nations taking arms against nations,

Constantly being bombarded with an inundation of falsification

And stereotypical implications

Fueling the box mentality and other foreseen and influenced
situations

But

I will no longer be intimidated by their intimidation

My

Free dome does not require permission

For ratification

It is- I am

After further investigation

Empowered to invoke cosmic transformation

I don't need any justification or validation

See

They still invade from office caves,

Clueless minds without an invitation

Digging deep into crevasses of thought formation

In an attempt

To control our 3rd density self-manifestations

Falling just short of decapitation

With forced indoctrination

Through music and tv stations

Institutions of education supported by doctored documentation

Which creates blinded misguided hybrid rebellion,

Societal acceptance, and assimilation

Making slaves without chains

Is power's ultimate demonstration

It's

Metaphorical and literal incarceration

See

The world needs a recalibration

To experience any true form of elation,

At any point in eternity's duration

We must except with open arms

Our physical and spiritual divination

Which

Requires self-reflection

Context, deep breathing, and complex contemplation

It might sound a bit crazy but

I think God is an abbreviation for

Imagination and meditation

Imagine the implications

Of what we could become

With a little focus and dedication

The

Self-appointed world rulers

Would be forced into abdication

Peace would bloom with light speed acceleration

Vanquishing, sickness, poverty, and every other form of
condemnation

And no one

Or administration

Would be the center of adoration

We are

The created creators of creation

You see dreams are merely the precursor to actualization,

The god you see, has always been there

Nestled deep in the recesses of the fertile mind

Patiently waiting

For activation

It's the only way to escape the simulation

Drink from the cosmic stream

Turn lead into gold

Become the alchemist

It's time for

Transformation.

INCHES

I often wonder

How many people I have offended?

I'm sorry if I did

I never meant it

It's funny how we reside in an ever-expanding universe-but

Live our entire lives playing a game of inches

And it's vicious

Or even sickening

Either way – this day in age—at this point in history

Those little lines of measurement can be the difference

Between sleeping in yachts or on park benches

Between love and hate

Life & death

Companionship and loneliness

Infidelity and friendship

What it looks like you're doing and

What's actually being done

What we think this is and the truth

A half inch here

A whole inch there can determine the quality of our existence

Believe it or not

We've been playing this self-defeating, self-limiting game since we were infants

But we can at least say

We've been consistently

Persistent

Pushing and pulling for validity and position

Crossing lines and straddling fences

Missing the fact—the point—the truth—and the reality of the matter by inches

And yards, and miles

From countries to towns

It's mere inches that separate smiles from frowns.

BEAUTY OF CHAOS

Together,

Rings of promise

Then matrimony

Through sickness and health

Honeymoon--repeatedly

Honey

moons

Seeds planted ... incubation

Apples fall like soon

Then another, then more

Dirty dishes

9 to 5

Toys & clothes all over the floor

Clean up, bedtime, expanded waist

Passion pushed to back burner/ on hold as life

Moves and shakes at a different pace

Dogs, cats, fish

Candles, cakes, make a wish

Games, concerts, and emergencies

Fights and arguments

Sleepovers and accidents

Puppy love and dances

Conversations like birds and bees

Heartbreak

Graduate

4 more yrs.

It's over they've flown the coop

Left with the emptiness

Of having an empty nest

Matrimony is

All that's left

Age

Quietly

The fruits of seeds now ride on laps

Mom is now mee maw and pop-pop becomes horseback

Quiet porch rocking as the sun sets

On the

Beauty of Chaos.

TRUTH

Eff a gun

The keyboard, The pen, the mic, and

My mind

Are the Roscoe/

Shooting potent shots

Of critical thinking

Into the minds and spines

Off the blind

Like armor piercing rounds

And Hollows

Manifesting

Words

Of

Healing and Freedom

That Take center stage

Never THE side Show,

Dropping

Heavy blows of cosmic sweet science

Which

alter perception

When

Landed in succession

Like a combo

Poetically

On a mission

To change

Cerebral conditions

Smacking the world into submission

Like Harpo

Turning dreams into reality

on life's canvas like Monet

with a touch Picasso

Its abstract

In fact

Roots run deep in the soil

Just like a live oak/

Shine the light on the darkness

Cultural appropriators and perpetrators

Just Like five-0

Essential

Aboriginal

Intertwined

With this American Tale

Just like FIEVAL

My passion

My pain

My

Determination is unbridled

Everybody looking at me

Looking at you

Like a recital

This game HAS nothing to do with winning It's about self-identification, legalese and SURVIVAL

Yeah, there are demons fighting against You —-us We all separated By money color And class It's all tribal

But you are your own Enemy Adversary n rival

You see Assassins assassinate leaders for being leaders, So you don't have to fear They won't find you I know A change gone come But til then let me remind you

That Superman and woman

Are real

But you don't need spandex and a cape

It's inside you

Every one of us

Gets emotional

True

But don't let it define you

Re focus

That energy

The results and outcomes

May ONE DAY

Surprise you

Because

Living by the seat of your pants

Only confines you ....

Leading to a plot or a cell

That they assign you

Overstand

God is the universe

Simply waiting

On you

to find you

To

Express—- your divinity

N Do all things

On Earth

As in heaven

Like you were

Designed to

Focus on the here and now

Not

What's behind you

Take your lessons

From the past

But never let it

Enshrine you

Transcend and transmute

The

Hate

Pain

Trauma

And abuse

And allow it to

Unwind n realign you

With

Light

Love

Gratitude

Compassion

If you can accept the

.... truth.......

PAUSE EXTENDED

Child

Born

Cry

Bottle

Watch

Touch—

Hot

Crawl

Walk

Gibber-jabber

Talk

Programmed

Trained thought still

Untaught

Inquisitive

Questions

Too young

Yet exposed

Teen

Still too young

Further exposure

Without disclosures

Rebellion

Why

More indoctrination

Those who aren't supposed to

Lie—

The have also been misinformed

Schools, and teachers unknowingly lie

Governments lie

Clear vision

Births confusion

Giving way to puberty

Then

Emotional turmoil

Knowing without knowledge

Search—seeking

Truth and understanding

Of self and surroundings

Meanwhile

People die

On tv, in music

On streets—at the hands of --

At home

In hospitals

People die

Because of why?

Cops, robbers, and heart attacks

After years of multi-cultural diverse diversions

Subversions

You realize

For the first time in real time

That – you are so called black

What a burden

Nigga

Where's the strap

We know exactly how to react

Desperately seeking ways out of this trap

Although

It's only a word

But most of us

Have become slaves to that

Adulthood

Now dreams are crushed

Adulthood

Realizing that the playing field isn't equal

For all of us

Hope turns to mush

With no path

Streets and badges kill your reflection

And imprison your soul

Digging into your subconscious without protection

And college is just another way of controlling

Us-regardless of complexion

But you

Ignore it

Push the fuck you and fuck it

Button

Long pause

In between

Now you straight

It wasn't too late

To reconfigure

Clean slate

You live the dream – in live stream

Spouse

Kids

Career

You—regurgitate

Your training

Washed & rinsed down even further

So, reality gets buried deeper

To keep up the delusion that

Real freedom was never murdered

Protection

Robotic

Until you see it

When you see it

If you see it

Long pause

You finally disconnect and unplug

Your mind from the paradigm

In order to realign

Cause you were blind

Realizing failure

Is just a sign to keep trying

Knowing that

Regardless of pills, swine or cops

Every day you live is another step towards dying

And every year

That passes look like the past

Until the future becomes the past

Blurring the lines of present time

Still searching

Still seeking

God or

Something to believe in

Age dawns

Often

Spawns' wisdom

For—some

Doctors

Pushing drugs

And shaky health

Truth

The end is near

No joy just fear—

You have

But the world

Never changed.

Maybe next time—because this time

The Pause is now a flatline.

THE USERS

Through hells fire and brimstone

I

Polish my skin tone

Remove the sword from my heart stone

To release a pain that's ingrown

Harness the power in my blood

Passed down from ancient cultures

And generations that been gone

Ready for war

I've taken knives, guns, spears, missiles, bombs and more and

Mumra'ed them into pen form

Used to uplift, admonish, and inform

Never question who I am

My allegiance has been sworn

Born where needs are dire

And streets used to be war torn

Where fathers sometimes vanish, and mothers been scorned

Where—

Some of the enemies look a like

While others

Perform in suits and uniforms

And after years of dedication to mental alteration

By minimalizing the support and education

Fierce altercations became a substitute for communication

So

Incarceration, poverty, and self-destruction is the only norm

But we helped create this storm

Now the future is muddled

It's hard to draw a line between right and wrong

Flashes of brilliance n opulence peak

In ball sports and writing songs

Producing seeds with no gratitude

Morally defunct-nonproductive-violent like demon spawns

Without a solid foundation because their parents and
grandparents gone

To work—or just gone

Because the og's have turned a blind eye

And have failed to perform

Idle minds and words

Turn to idle arms

Under this spell of faux unity

Diplomacy and lucky charms

Racial tension is the illusionary norm

But it can be stopped

My only question is

Are we as a society too far gone?

Unaware

Active participation in the subliminal plantation only makes it strong

Now the masters sit in corporate chairs

And the employees are still hands on the farm

Deceived to believe things have changed

But current times reveal

Shits been the same all along

Figure heads hustle us into remaining calm

While so called spiritual leaders

Advise us to be patient and strong

That

A man dressed like a terrorist will eventually come along

Then what

March and pray

Like yesterday and today

That the horned

Has mercy and doesn't bring us more harm

I know

Most of us don't play chess

Yet we all have become pawns

Thots and johns

Subjected to the unprotected sodomization

Of a nation's ongoing con

So, what's the solution?

Is self-love and self-education the key to unravelling the illusion?

What's it going to take to destroy our self-hate and ease the
tension and confusion?

I look around and see promise like

We are no longer in collusion

Have we reach a point in time where we quit cold turkey?

Pumping these insane ways and ideas into our hearts and brains
we been abusing?

Or

Do we keep using?

DON'T LOOT

Listen

Black people

I know most of us believe

In

An eye for an eye or

Tooth for a tooth

But here is a bit a truth

We can march, we can protest in outrage

As is our right but why

Do we have to Loot?

Providing context and pretext

For them to aim and shoot

Solidifying our image

And providing

Further justification

For what they do to you

I know your hurt and your tired

Of being under barrels, knees and boots,

But

All the violence and damage where u live at

renders your point,

your conversations

And your intentions mute,

We should shout,

We should March in outrage

We should Protest

But you don't have to loot

Your anger

Is justified

But the strategy needs to be modified

You are are destroying the livelihood in some cases

Of people who look like you

I know it's frustrating

And

It's hard to know what to do,

But I implore you

Don't spend your money in their businesses,

Pool it for political power

And dismantle the old infrastructure

Every time you have an opportunity

In the voting booth,

But

Think

don't loot

Hold the line

But don't loot,

March, protest, scream, shout, clog the streets,

But don't loot

Plan, organize, and strategize

To accomplish the mission

We can no longer tolerate these conditions

Too many senseless unjustified deaths

And not enough convictions

But looting only strengthens their position

We got they attention

The civil unrest

The descension

Don't allow the rioters and looters

To distract from the goal

To knock injustice

And racism

Completely out of commission

So

March

Protest

Scream

Shout

Express your anger,

Spread our truth

But please

On everything I love

Which includes you

Please

DONT LOOT!!

LET'S GET SOME COFFEE

Dear Mr. And Mrs. So called White man

How can one pull himself up by his bootstraps if he or she only has one hand?

So, with all sincerity

Fuck your skewed poll numbers & economic disparity

I just need real opportunity, not your poor thing charity

And for clarity,

Fuck the guise of white privilege and white power

Fuck your so-called slavery and the ship you rode in on

Fuck your implied superiority

Fuck the black codes, White Leagues, and Jim crow

Fuck the cointel pro and Fuck hangings

Fuck ghettos

Fuck the years you been handing out after you gave us the means for slanging

Fuck your holier than thou complex

Fuck survival of the fittest and evolution

Fuck the biased one-sided curriculums in those sheep herding zombie making institutions

Fuck your refusal to understand-sympathize-comprise or institute solutions

Fuck your fear of my so-called black skin

Have you ever considered that

Maybe I feel the same way when you walk in

Fuck you Patty and Karen

Fuck police brutality

And the years of propaganda making people of color the enemy

Fuck your documented historical violence

And your complicit silence

That you conveniently try to erase from memory

Fuck race riots and the word nigger

You will no longer be my boogie man

I don't hate you—and fuck anyone who thinks that I do.

We fear the same fears as you

All I want to do is live as free and as prosperous as you think you do

Stress free and comfortably

Softly and gaudy

Together or alone,

Now let's get some coffee.

PROBLEMS P1

The problem with problems

Is

They will always be problems

Everybody wants to talk about them

But nobody wants to really solve them

Especially when they under the impression

That the problems as they stand

Involves them

Even if it's only by default

I wish the whole woe is me syndrome would end or just halt

Victimless victims cry out in hate

With a mouth full of sea salt

To the point where their words come out of they face

Sounding like hee haw

Standing in the middle of everything

Whole body playing see saw

The reality is reality tv and what we can buy at the mall

Y'all

Our problems

Have masked themselves as someone else's fault

As a result

Self-accountability is in a constant free fall

Constantly shaming others for their short comings

Playing tag your it

Or some twisted game of leapfrog

How doesn't matter

Now

All they need is a name

Even when the solution smacks them in the face

Like a runaway train

They never saw coming

Never knowing when to quit

Running in circles—heart constantly pumping

Chasing they own tails or they're white whale

Til they die in the ring at the hands of Dolph Lundgren

Ain't that something

Black, red, white, brown, yellow

The mindset, and problems are all the same

Look close

The have and have nots are on the same field

But are definitely- not playing the same game

Yet and still

It's all the same game

And life becomes strange

When your closest girlfriends or homies wake up and try to change

It's on them

That you still standing in place

So, it's their fault that they became lame

They got lucky

It was never a talent or brains

Living off memories and picture frames

Harping on loses not gains

Where people become sell outs because they

Chose a different path and

Choose to drive their car in a different lane

Where queen aren't queens

They not even women

Just labeled thots and dames

Problems will always be problems

Until we acknowledge

The real blame

CAN'T GET ALONG

Now you See

What you see

Now

Is not new to me,

it's not unfamiliar

My kind has dealt

With atrocities of this magnitude

And beyond

For .... Well....

let's just say a long time...

If you go back to like the 50s, 60s, 70s, 80s, 90s and beyond --TIL now

It's a shame

Because

What you'll find is

that

The social commentary hasn't changed

Slavery maybe even Jim Crow

Has visually stopped

But the disdain for my people

Has not

So, neither has the black man's, especially the black man's

attitude, his fear of being accused, arrested for nothing,

And slain by the cops

For

Walking or driving while black in a nice car, nice clothes

In the wrong neighborhood or along his own road or his block,

I know your probably thinking

Like black's people kill each other all the time

But

whites, Asians, and Latinos do too

The only difference between us and you

Is that it's NOT always

On the news

And just like you and yours

Him and theirs

some of us do stupid shit

But that

Doesn't mean all of US should be abused

Check it

How would you feel

If we truly blamed all of you for all things your ancestors, racist cops, and politicians did and still do,

And please don't look confused—

With that I don't get or didn't realize attitude,

It's a played-out ruse,

And if I was you, I'd be nervous too

Cuz it's a wonder it took this long for the men and women of color to finally blow a fuse,

Social media is a gift and a curse,

A platform for racist, coons, all forms of entertainers and socialites, educators, politicians and buffoons,

But social injustices are being posted now too

And starting to get all the views,

Because currently the mainstream media

Can no longer control everything

we consume,

Now you see

What we've seen for way too long

Maybe now you got a glimpse

Of why we

All

just can't get along

DON'T MOVE

My hands are up

So, don't shoot

As I--we stew in this toxic soup

Of innocence, guilt, and spoiled fruits

Getting hit from both sides and all angles,

By the mis-informed old heads and the incorrigible youth

Who've been over emotionalized, sensitized, and psychologically captured by the

Inundation of fictious material that has been intentionally set loose

On an unassuming population like a biblical plague of Zeus,

But don't shoot—

We've been lured, into the lap of the trap

Perhaps meant to distract

While being overlapped by the comforting sounds of the piper's magical flute

Intentions hidden and redacted

Without transparency

Apparently subdued

Please don't shoot

My hands are up

Not because I surrender, but because I'm fed up

With being hated, shot, and suffocated by non-law-abiding citizens that push the legal limits, and the policy backed municipal troops

Fueled by a system that carries shackles and an invisible Neuse,

Truth, they all spooked by the spook

Alone and in groups

T-shirt or Hooded— on foot— in Nikes and Timberland boots,

pushing a nice ride—luxury jeep or coup— regardless of the style of commute

Just my presence can bring pressure from Karen's and Grunts with badges and blue suits

It's like--

The mere site--Incites a chemical imbalance that replaces common sense with a sense of fear

Which Induces verbal and physical abuse--

Status quo, monthly bonuses, and political statistics to boot--

But fuck all that-- don't shoot,

Caught in a constant loop of swarthy skin equals guilt without proof-

Don't move—my hands are up in protest

Don't move—You asked for my wallet

My insurance is in my arm rest—don't move-

Don't you take another step-or take your last breath

Don't move—your skin requires no respect

Choke hold-knee on neck—you are not allowed to refute

Don't move—or else they will shoot

EPIPHANY

Lost in a vortex

Stemming from a mental complex

Created in a vacuum of

Misperception, deception, verbal definitions and presented out
of context

Spawned from the metaphorical poison injected into the hippo
campus, thalamus, limbic system, and cerebral cortex

To the effect that we see

Man, and god as two diametrically opposed concepts

As if hot and cold, spirit and flesh

Arent't one in the same breath

Like the sun doesn't rise in the east and set in the west

And still

We haven't seen more than one sun yet

Its

Time for the minds of humankind to be reprogrammed,
recalibrated, and reset

Retrained, and drilled

Until self-realization, gratitude, understanding and peace are a
reflex

You see

The invisible weapons pointed at our brains have been engrained
since before our days at recess, and

Should be considered a deep threat

A form of terrorism and pretext

Of war cloaked under the words

Entertainment and the internet

And it will continue

If we don't interject and use cosmic wisdom and intellect

Like Enoch, Ibrahim, and Melchizedek

You are the children of the most high

Your ancestral strength and power are limitless

Overstand this

Even in the belly of the beast

That concrete jungle like hell

An allegorical wilderness

Filled with poverty stricken, dysfunctional families, and crime
riddle communities like the us

You are the singularity and the assembly

So, stand strong and fear less

Smile in the face of your enemies physically and mentally

For who you are is not a dream

This is not conjecture or an illusion

This truth spoke as a symbolic symphony

Of cerebral ambrosia n verbal soliloquy

So, open your eye...accept your divinity

And let this be

Your

Epiphany

.... Now wake the f#@k up!!

PEACE

Is it peace?

Or a piece

That brings peace

Or does the fear of not having- peace

Keep it just beyond our reach

Like trying to touch a sunset

While standing on a beach

Just a little something I ponder

Before my rare moments of silence are leached.

And as I lay me down to sleep

The endorphins slowly release

The muck of the day quickly falls into retreat

My consciousness fades away into the deep

Awaken state located somewhere

Between the vast unknow

And the comforting folds of my cold sheets

Nothing happens

It's still

Until I impregnate the realm with questions

To receive the answers, I seek

My very being expands and I start to understand

Why some call me a freak

But I won't ever weep

Weak never

How is it my fault

I can peak behind the veil and see what's right in front of us

Right in front of me

I refuse to accept the bleak

Its why the dead seldom rest

And lives are so incomplete—and why

There are so many players in the game

That are unprepared to compete

Tormented by the illusion of struggle

And marred by the perception of defeat

Chasing an idea of freedom

That only can be achieved with

Determination

Contemplation and the loss of conceit

The first stage of victory

Is knowing instead of belief

Self-realization can expose the falsehood of time

So that now just becomes

Making forever

What is often so brief....

NOTHING

People

Have childlike tantrums or

Adult like emotional conniptions

In and out of

Precarious positions

Becoming victims

Of they own pains and symptom producing conditions

Due to guilt and other forms of

Self-mental infliction

Their diagnosis and prescriptions have become distorted

Common sense completely aborted

By the rapid influx of

Cortisol and adrenaline

Lexapro and Ritalin

Zoloft and Adderall

Weed, coke, and alcohol

Flooding an already emotionally weak system

Turning a passing moment

Into a lifelong addiction, death, or conviction

It's almost as if

It's your life's mission

To breed

Misery and dissention

Instead of cultivating love and prevention

At any second

Any one thing or combination

Can serve as a lynchpin

Becoming a release valve for your external combustion

Yelling,

Throwing hands,

Knives,

And guns

For what most of the time is

Nothing...

<u>SHHHHhhhhh!</u>

I thought

Before I could

Or knew I was

And now I am

Because I know.

CELESTIAL ECHO

Question:

What if you were God?

Answer:

I am...

DEFEAT

Strength

Isn't necessarily proven by

Empty victories

But rather is

Forged in the fiery pits of defeat

Like two opponents in the street

It's where,

Getting knocked down and getting up meet

Even when the climb is steep

You can rest

But don't you ever retreat

For it is here

That you are urged to dig deep and reach

For that next level and then the next

Pushing beyond your limit

Until you have obtained your peak

See

To achieve real victory

You must first experience, endure, and overcome

Defeat.

INNOCENCE

When does innocence-

Lose its innocence

In

What instance—

Does its purity

Become--

Clouded with muck, spots, and blemishes...

Then

Bloats and leaks from all corners

Then

Without any sense of awareness

Innocence-

Becomes intimately entangled

and

Indistinguishable

From ignorance

Or /and

Marred by repetitive instances that

emotionally charge outrage and resentments--

That

Transform innocence into all out disgust & Militance-

Spawning generations of disrespectful

Unintelligent belligerence

That has been

Drenched in the stench

& Steady drip of filth

That slips through the passcodes and parental advisory stickers

To the point

That,

Even the idea of Innocence loses its sentiment

No need for deliberation

The past & present provide

Sufficient evidence

that

Your mental and physical--

Abuse, mutilation, and demise

Are—

Probable—streamed live—

& Therefore eminent-

Unfortunately--

This --

Is still a predicament

So

How do we maintain the natural Innocence?

Do you

Allow yourself to plunge deeper

Into that bottomless hole that cajoles your soul

Further into the suffering darkness

Or do you lash out

With lassos of resilience

Do you turn the other cheek-?

Get on your knees to ask for reprieve & forgiveness or

Turn, face and finish it

Stand firm or

Allow the firm to render you impotent

What good is millions and billions of dollars

If you can't pop bottles

And hollow point words that convey your

Power and brilliance...

Feed the homeless—help the less fortunate

its

God's resemblance

That's

Been hung, stab, shot, and dragged behind a curtain—

To smother your luminance-

Beaten over the head & left for dead—

by

Some invisible hand

Holding a blunt instrument

To

Keep us blind and trembling

Confuse the languages and tip the scales of intelligence

To

push the irrelevant into relevance

to

blur the lines

so, you can't tell the difference between

Wickedness and innocence

To make sure we are all imbued with some since of guiltiness.

But where is the resistance

Bills generate-

But the only one due is diligence

When did innocence?

Seeing, breathing,

Speaking

Or just being

become so F@#king

scary and menacing?

We are sentient

God and Flesh Symbionts

When did innocence?

And the innocent

Stop being innocent?

PRAYING FOR BEFORE

Dismayed

As bullets sprayed

See shells laid – next to

Laid n scattered at different angles

In warm cold flesh --Laid

Motionless on the paved

Lodged deep in walls,

car doors,

and graves

Lodge deep in mother's mind as she prayed

To relive the former better days

When---

He, she, they, we played

Without fear of being hanged or sprayed

Before

He, she, they, we

Embodied and embraced

Hood, Thug, Dealer. Wish a nigga would, Bitch ass nigga

&

Slave.

STOP IT

In a world of a billion

Unfamiliar - familiar faces

Residing in familiar and unfamiliar/public and obscure places

I ask

How can anyone have the Gaul/

The FUCKING

Audacity to be a Bigot I meant Racist

It's tasteless

And rests on facts that are baseless,

Serving only to solidify that out here-out there somewhere

In this gigantic bubble -Where

Masses of people are lazy

And their minds are still childlike, rudimentary

And basic

Like it's hard to walk and chew gum at the same time kind of

Basic

You know?

As if we don't breathe the same air

Go to the same schools

Work at the same jobs

Or live in the same hoods

I mean face it

We are not going anywhere

And

This didn't just happen

Either

It's always been this way

I mean

We are all plugged into the same system

I meant crammed into the same box,

With the top wired shut with metal braces—

And bricked OVER by stone MASONS

I mean we've always occupied the same spaces

So, I've asked myself for years—let's just say ages

How can anyone have the Gaul

The FUCKING audacity,

The Hutzpah to be Racist

I mean people that are not of the ...

–PERSUASION-

Have always been subjected to being subjects

Treated like cattle and objects

Beaten, killed, raped, and tossed into ghettos and then projects

------Right?

I mean their exploits have Conquered and populated the four corners of the known earth...

Under the auspices of the crown or the church

On soul saving missions

I'm amused that the people you've presumably kept under your shoes for thousands of years are a threat to your position—

Right next to me...

I ask

What did another group of people do that promogulated this passed down tradition?

That mind state of Hate...

I'll wait.

There must be something or

Maybe there isn't

You just woke up one day and your mind was in prisoned by bright clouds of darker faces scattered throughout the so-called races—

And who invented that word?

Its utterly absurd...but we hang on it

But I digress

I am still waiting

Debating to myself that you really don't have an answer...none of
you do---

And if its jealousy then ok—but

I'll do you one better

It's actually rather clever

How someone not you of course—

Attempted to reconstruct and reimagine the history so no one
could find it EVER.

-and therein lies the joke—

How do you hide something from a n.i.g.g.a?

Books ha-ha

Suddenly the idea of truth finds the face of the surf—

And then the hypothesis

Everything in His-story

Happened in reverse.

No seriously-think about it

I know I know

In your mind that is beyond perverse

Unless

Picture this "black panther party" civil rights movement and then

KKK and the White league....

Interesting...

If that wasn't enough here is another clue....

Maybe you were under some else's shoe...TOO

Either way it's NOT right....

In my understanding of life its despicable to hate someone off site...

Or fright....

It often ignites the plighted to get up and fight...

Or maybe You they were just sick and tired of not being fully represented or just tired of working the fields in the hot sun for nothing

Being poor and downtrodden

And much like now

Insignificant and forgotten

To the spoiled rotten powers

Feeding and devouring everything off the backs of yours and ours

It's crazy to think that

We are metaphorically the Same---

Related by little codes of DNA that are regulated by choices

In 3 generations your great grandkids could look like me

And vice versa

So, neighbor, embrace it

I am going end the same way I began

I ask

How can anyone have the Gaul/

The FUCKING

Audacity

The chutzpah

to be a Bigot

I meant Racist

In a world of a billion

Unfamiliar - familiar faces

Separation is a mirage and microscopic

Just Stop it.

IS IT ME

It would seem

That—

Within the assumed

Unconfined parameters of the American Dream

That-

My Greatest Enemy is Me

But why?

Practically--- I mean --

Basically

At the very foundation-

My whole life—

Everything comes down to Me-

Yet-- I'm

Lost like a ship at sea,

Living,

In what I surmise, can only

Be

Someone else's reality,

Where—

After we escape the confines of our mother's lake-

The

Idea of Self—

Becomes a casualty –

In order to be

Assimilated and fully integrated into the matrix

I meant this fantasy

That

Extends beyond the far reaches of what a

"Hu-man" can see

Elaborately Housed under a fictious canopy

Of literal & metaphorical insanity

Narrated by mainstream broadcast conglomerates

Puppeted by THE group behind the curtain-

An oz like confeder-acy

Using arcane arts to impart despotism & fear

Hidden behind the guise of legality

Void of morality-

It's got to be some form of -criminality

To

Keep the world spinning in a cycle of incessant CARNALITY

That

Cements the illusion-

And

Perpetuates this air of confusion

between land and sea-

(HEAVEN & HELL)

Between YOU and ME

Making bulls think they're cows,

N cows think they're bulls –

While turning proverbial sharks into MANATEES,

Feeding the pulse of superficiality

While

Constructing glass ceilings that limit

what we can achieve—

Then

Deceived-

To believe-

What we are given to

Perceive

We all live with a sense of franticality-

With undertones of self-imposed suicide –

Through what we inject & consume in totality

And threats of violent physicality

which

Induces stress and anxiety-

That's injected into the veins of society

To

Kill any potential hope and thoughts of Joviality

Doubling down on the – keep foot on neck syndrome/

Altering the meaning of what it is to "BE ----FREE"

Demonizing knowledge and

Suppressing spirituality

To

Keep us disconnected and engaged in misshapen acts of sexuality

–

Lowering vibrations with over promotion

Of 2 legged beastiality,

Ostracized and Criticized ---especially

If your mentality

Doesn't appear to conform to the sanctioned form of –
Normality

Which-

Only functions to forge cookie cutter knock-offs-

And to stifle and discourage Originality

Blurring the lines until

We can't tell the difference between

Fact and Fiction-

You see

Little things like the word RACE (for example)

Are merely a formality

A conscious attempt to destroy blood ties & commonality

So, everyone is a stranger with no notion of familiarity

And it's not just me or You this is happening

With a global Universality

So, everyone thinks they are alone-prone to feelings of

disparity

I'm constantly asking questions

strategically

To find solutions that dispel the delusion

But No one answers me

Fixated on the aura I created

Most gaze upon me crazily

But what if I'm not

As if these statements weren't just pulled out of thin air

And working for a boss- I mean an owner- at an office- I meant a
Farm – I mean for Wages isn't Slavery--

Please

Don't judge too hastily

For every action has some sort of reaction,

In simple terms-

The law of causality

All the mayhem to distort & scramble

The cosmic signals that power our innate faculties

But maybe—

I am a bit off kilter

And Maybe

Within the assumed

Confined-Unconfined parameters of this Hologram- The
American Dream

That-

My Greatest Enemy is Me

SELF-MASTERY

Under this

Canopy that

We have

Conveniently and systematically

Labeled

Humanity

Has, for centuries, been

Essentially

Possessed, encapsulated, and oppressed,

By this

Pervading narcissistic demonic spirit of greed and vanity

Feeding off the induced states of lower vibrational frequencies

While

Being consistently plunged into the deep throws of an ongoing
calamity

Steeped in this murky infusion of horror-scifi- multidimensional
fantasy

A sort of twisted Shakespearean dramady

Where

The now is

Tethered at the ankle to the past

And the future

Is blocked by walls covered in stab masks, fear, and brutality

So the present—is no longer the gift we'd have it be

(shit) it's barely classified as reality

With programs programming, reprogramming, and streamlining
our mentalities

Stoking the smoke that overshadows most –making surviving
and thriving baffling

Challenging our health, the Physical and mental,

To dampen the rise of our inherent spirituality

With the poisonous nature of constructed social paradigms,
obscenities, acute toxicity,

It's profanity

Steadily repeating and reproducing these circular cycles of
insanity

That

Destabilizes communities, whole countries, corrupts politicians,
and destroys families

Striking with simplistic complexity

Using subtle deviations in the panoply

It's a tragedy

When people are forced to react

Out of hopelessness, and disparity

Cause finances crashed, or dreams were dashed

And ideologies are reduced to picket signs and hastags

Due to the lack of clarity--

Cerebral shores, harbors, and villages are

Invaded pillaged and enslaved

By psychological barbarity

Followed by dastardly acts of savagery

Committed by the over-zealous, thugs, cretons and misfits and

Exemplified when 911 only calls in the Calvary

And this exists

Just under the surface of all the pomp and pageantry

Behind the curtain of the wizard's ima--gery

Just outside the realm of flattery,

Look, we've been beaten

Drastically

Imitated and enshrined,

Murdered and confined

Almost magically

Only to be preserved and observed through the translucent walls

Of a glass menagerie,

Emphatically colored within the lines of

A global masterpiece

Subjected to being subjected

Until we uncover the secrets of

SELF- MASTERY....

YOU N I VERSE

From deep within

The You n I verse -- You n I verse,

Often merging as one

Yet, I exist

Because

You give birth and it hurts

Gift or curse – only adds

A priceless tag to your worth

As I grow in

Knowledge and wisdom

I

Come to understand that you

Were there before the beginning

And

still deserve to be first

And it was love at first sight

Enamored by your resilience, strength, and depth

I'm fully Immersed

In your beautiful light

Whose brilliance is only magnified by your voice

Vibrating in angelic verse

igniting an insatiable appetite

That burns day and night

And only gets worse as I

Long for the moments that

You n I verse

It's the only time

Mind and emotions come together and burst

Quenching all versions of thirst

Rekindling the memories

That

You are the creator of

Life, the sun, moon, stars

And the Earth

A Vast Infinite Stream Of cosmic organic genius

That

Inspires, tickles, and flirts

Whenever

You n I verse

In an on going

cyclic cycle

Of lasts and first

Life is worth every minute that

You and I verse

Unrehearsed converse at length or in spurts

Your visage becomes my church

My psychologist and my nurse

Causing dark clouds to disperse

Freeing my mind in space and time to ponder

if death and life are happening in reverse

you are my love, you are my destiny

life takes on a new meaning, whenever

You and I verse.

THRILLED

We-- Fell in love long before we meet

I didn't know you and you didn't know me

We--Exchanged energy well before being intimate

We--You and me

Separated by land and sea--externally

So--How could this be—I meant we

I wonder if we knew before

Would we still have taken the same roads or chased the same
dreams

And if this was always going to be the result

Why did we have to go through everything in between?

The math doesn't math

We come from two different backgrounds and places

Following separate paths

Until worlds collided en masse—

forcing us to pick up the shards of shattered glass

From past situations that didn't last, and it happened fast

almost drove us mad- and it was sad--to the point where

Happiness became a mask to hide the pain and the contents of my flask.

Before taking actions that seemed rash-

It was like tightly holding onto the seatbelt seconds before the crash,

But, before I could blink, I, we, there you were there in a flash

So, I ask

Is this divine will or the work of divine wills?

Or a soul separated only to be reunited at last or

Two celestial bodies

Gravitationally hurled towards one another to be fulfilled.

I pinch myself daily, So I know that its real

I don't know how we got here; I just know how it feels

And I am thrilled.

THE LAST ROUND

Sweat drips

Stinging

The cut above my eye

As I suckle my swollen lip

Doubt creeps in

Now I question if I'm really equipped

to barrel through the pain

And this so-called human wall of bricks

That seems to foil my every attempt,

Absorbing my every hit,

Who's up on the score cards,

I think I'm getting my ass whipped,

I never thought I'd feel the day

My opponent would catch my slip,

I see my corner man's mouth moving

But right now, I don't hear shit

I can't tell whether he is yelling for the sake of yelling

Or feeding me tips,

But I can't keep my eyes off the conundrum

Across the ring from me

That's been giving me fits

But I got to calm down

Take deep breaths....

I'm shaking

But only a little bit

I pray nobody can see me losing my grip

Ding, ding

There goes the bell

Another swing of Agua,

Damnit it hurts to spit,

Why am I doing this?

For the fame, the glam or the glitz

For the ring side groupies

Man they be all my.....

Or because I want to be money Mayweather rich

I thought I had this

But every movie has its twist

to hell with it

The why doesn't matter

Cuz I effin love this shit

Mouth peace in

For all the marbles, frankly this is it,

I stand

Lights shine

I fell off the bike for a second

Now it's time to get back in the mix

Camera's flicker,

The screaming crowd grows into a whisper,

Time to be the heavy hitter

I was born for this

My folks ain't raise no quitter

Last round

3 mins

I got to go for the game winner

98 Jordan

Final seconds I got to stick this game winner

After this

It's got to be red lobster, Sizzler

somewhere expensive for dinner

Bullseye,

Deadshot,

Hawk eye

C. Ferrell, Will Smith

J. Renner

This is the last round

I will be victorious

I am not going down

But it's going down

I channel the spirit of greatness

Holyfield

Tyson

Lewis

Foreman

Sugar Ray

Haggler

Hearns

Ali

De la

Money may

Jones

B Hopkins

Whitaker

Forman

and more

To

Take me to the crown

I will be victorious

In this the

Final round

DIVINE LIGHT

I am Divine

in body, soul, and in mind

A sublime truth

I discovered

After I realized my programming glitched--which

Used to kept me

In a state of constant flux and decline,

Like superstar athletes after their prime

But it's crazy how

A little reading and a little me time

Can uproot your whole conscience perspective,

So, you have to shift and realign

With the light that shines up the 33 step like vertebrae of your spine,

A steep climb

That send you hurling through the 700 trillion plus universal star cells

To find

That the great architect of the un I verse

The creator is self-created

And that your world is yours

and mine world is mine

Unveiling this false cloak of outside intangibles,

That keep us drugged up and locked behind mental cages like animals

Afraid to draw and color outside of the lines

Meaning you have been shuffling the deck, and

Dealing your own hands

This whole -entire -time,

You see divine

We are light reflected

Dim-because we have failed to see what we have neglected,

Choosing not to listen to that little voice we've been instructed to reject

Ignoring the little gems that you unknowingly introspect

So, you think the word nigga and brutality

Is the highest form disrespect – yet

You think you got off a boat with no history and this the trickery you will accept

Like the information provided is meant to keep you astute and abreast,

Like the emergency broadcast system

This life is a test

and you don't have to wake-up

If you haven't slept...

But I digress

We are not this flesh its only there to keep the real you protected

Under and Overstand Divine

You are light reflected.

WITHOUT CHANGE

We

Talk a lot of SHIT!

About a lot of Shit

Kicks,

3s and dunks,

Chips

And songs we dropped

Bout

How we make it rain from the bricks we flipped,

The hot new rims we just slapped on our whip,

How. Much ass and gas we hit

And let's not forget how everything and everyone is lit

We can go from zero to ten

Quick

How much time we got

After we beat that nigga ass or left a nigga

Stiff - Swift

To pop shit

About how Karen and nem got us pissed

About the state we in

How the cops keep increasing they level of bulshit

And how we are dying because of it

How the man still hasn't loosened his vice grips

And,

America's unfortunately evident racist shit

Because

We supposed to be on some free shit

Shit, I love us, and what we idealistically represent

but I'm sick of this

Blame everybody else instead of ourselves,

Trust and believe I know they play a part

But I ain't talking about them

I'm talking about us

When do we take responsibility for our own shit?

Pull up our big boy draws and panties on some real grown shit,

We talk a lot

For a group of people that don't own shit,

Won't pool resources to establish some throne shit,

Go for the throat

Or at least pay the right mother fuckers so we can demand shit
for our vote

I can't stand this

I am not going to read I'll just go along with whatever the
deceivers told us to believe,

Because its easy, and its they fault, the system is rigged, and it is

But financial freedom is a tease

So, I will just keep my head down, work, or not, and cry for help

because I don't have knowledge of self and I can hide behind
these street creds and degrees,

And for the most part I mind my business because the society's
problems don't have nothing to do with me,

Until it does, and one of yours or one of mine

Is addicted to drugs or becomes a thug

Then we want to open our lips

March, protest, throw all out fits

And talk more shit

Without change

Pardon me

For thinking

Critically

Analytically

Metaphorically

In simile, and hyperbole

Intelligently

& Abstractly

When as a matter of fact

We don't usually

Yet,

we are unafraid to prove that we are brave

don't take no shit or what we perceive as disrespect

So, either its jail for losing control-or protecting that rep we made

Maybe protecting our set

or

here lies so and so and he wasn't no punk

Inscribed on his grave,

PARDON ME

THE BIG PICTURE

For most niggas

Your niggas

My niggas

Dope niggas

Square niggas

Round niggas

These niggas

Those niggas

Hot niggas

Cold niggas

Real niggas

Bitch made niggas

Life exposes all niggas

This—Living hell

Stokes fires to roast niggas

Alive

To--strengthen their position over niggas

While powerful invisible hands

Threat choke & metaphorically hold niggas

To death and in place

Visually and audibly terrorizing to stress and rattle niggas

Baffled niggas

Put they lives on the shelf

With no direction or realization of self

But it's all calculated into the figures

Like niggas can't get ahead because as a whole

Have been presumably cut off from the wealth

So making fast cash is the thoughts of mad niggas

Out here

Robbing

Pulling burners

And killing other niggas that look like themselves or another
nigga

Never seeing the larger picture

Niggas

Out here

Blaming other niggas

For their lack of dividends

For their station or position and their failure to see how this
grand chess board is configured

Relying on other niggas

White and government niggas

Instead of being a self-sufficient nigga

Nigga

You see ignorance is bliss

Is a concept I wish

Didn't exist

Notice how that same unawareness

Works out for the fish

Making a tasty dish

But niggas don't want to hear shit from me or another nigga

Especially if he not a in the hood doing good or a broke nigga

just not a larger-than-life flashy type nigga

Or a baller nigga

Most niggas idolize the wrong type of niggas

Killah niggas

Dope boy niggas

I got to stick my dick in every hole kind of nigga

And want to be thug type niggas

Well

Show me the real picture nigga

Show me your future nigga

Will you be a free nigga?

That live in a big house nigga

Or in the big house nigga

Are you a sky is the limit type nigga?

Or they are holding me down type nigga

Maybe you're 6 feet under the ground type nigga

Can you explain to me?

What is a real nigga vs a fake nigga?

All I want is for you to think about it nigga

Rationalize it nigga

Internalize it nigga

Destroyed the whole concept of a victimized nigga

Take your feelings out of this shit--nigga

So, you can see the game and,

The big picture....

CATHARTICUM

Breath in--

I was trained

To absorb & to normalized exuberant amounts of pain

Simplified— we've been

Victimized by a down pour

Of falsified and misleading claims

Bolstered by years of traumatic fears

Lethally and unequally injected between the eyes and behind the
ears

I meant ingrained

Triggering an automatic

Upload into the very fabric

of our genetic mainframe —

Downloaded, and integrated,

Into the DNA codes of every one of our subsequent generations

Since the Sephardic and Moors--surrendered al Andalusia or

what you refer to as Spain

Altering ancestral memories and names

Disrupting the links to the greatness

Still Coursing through our veins

While-- fracturing and segmenting what remains of our brains

And thwarting all attempts to reconnect those chains

Resulting in senseless violence, run on sentences, graves,
underachievement and shame

Masked as pride

Based on complicit menticide

That has

Cascaded down through decades like droplets of rain

Deep inhale

Once sacred—our mothers, daughters, and sisters are
disrespected, neglected and over sexualized

Men and boys--well

Chemically castrated and effectively neutralized

Criminalized so assassinations are seemingly incentivized,
legalized, and televised

The roles of Femininity and masculinity have been usurped and
switched

Whole families have been destroyed by deceptive programming
and the flick of the wrist,

Shit Everyone is at risk

One plate,

One drink,

One pill,

One blunt away from being mortally sick,

We have officially been terrorized.

Suffocated &

Destabilized

In hopes that we die quick

Despised

Left only with the will to survive.

But Exhale—

Because there is a twist

Brewing In the midst of this fiery pit

See

We have to learn that

Even in the midst

We must let go of all this--

Superficial and mundane shit

It doesn't matter, it never mattered

And that's

To say the least

You can't solve intentionally crafted problems

The solution is out of reach

Until we use the right weapons and properly storm the right beach

Your participation is just a mechanism that feeds the beast

Exhale

I have found peace

Looking behind the curtain to

Converse with the wise

Armed with knowledge

my eyes spy another level

Giving the dead the spirit to rise

To meet the devil, this Satan, this adversary, toe to toe—Eye to Eye

Forcing the structure of this material and patrilineal matrix

To abate and Dematerialize

A peace

Dripped from the cosmos

Revealing what the illusion of suffering is meant to symbolize

Forcing me to realize

That

This contrast and struggle are just a way,

To not only obtain

But to appreciate your prize

Especially when you are blind

Blind to the outer and inner God's design

Exhale and let your light shine

Exhale and release your emotional ties to this fictitious disguise

That draws us closer to our demise

Perpetuating this no hope vibe

While the key to unlock you has been buried deep inside

Exhale

Let it all go and thrive

Remember every story has two sides

And you are realized in every part of them

At the end and the start of them

So inhale the stress, and the pain of now and past

Exhale and let it all go and let this be your

Catharticum.

Thank you for taking the time to read this book. I truly appreciate your open-mindedness. Thank you for assimilating the information whether you agree or not, and whether it touches you or not. Know it or not, you have opened neurological pathways that could lead to higher states of thinking analytically, while broadening your perspectives. My sincere hope is that this book inspires reflection and creativity. I hope it expands and deepens the conversation internally and socially.

Thank you, thank you, thank you.